Ben Gets

Storie
Ann Jun

Illustrate
Tony Mo

PURNELL

Ben and his mum went into the shop.
The shop had a funny door.
''I want to go round and round,''
shouted Ben.
''Come on!'' said Mum. ''That's enough.''

They went on the escalator.
''Ben, hold my hand tightly,'' said Mum.
''There are so many people. If you don't hold tight, you might get lost.''
''Not me!'' said Ben.

They went to the book department.
The next department was full of toys.
There were electronic games. There
were building bricks and spacemen.

Mum stopped to buy a book. Ben looked at the electric train. Then he looked at the wagons and the signals and the signalmen. He let go of Mum's hand.

Suddenly the lift opened. Lots of people rushed out. Ben looked for his mum, but he couldn't see her.

''I'll go back to the books,'' thought Ben. ''Mum will find me there.'' Ben looked for the books, but he could only see shoes. He was lost.

He walked past hats. He walked past coats and dresses. He walked past towels. He walked past cups and saucers.

"I can't find the books," thought Ben. "And I can't find Mum." All he could see were pockets. Pockets in coats and pockets in men's jackets.

Mum went to the toy department.
She stood near the train.
''He's not here,'' she thought. ''He
must be lost.''

Mum went to the assistant.
''Have you seen my little boy?'' she asked. ''He was looking at the train.''
''They all do,'' said the assistant.

Ben knew he was lost. The shop was full of big people, all in a hurry. Ben began to cry. Then he yelled, "I want my mum!"

A kind lady spoke to him.
''Have you lost your mum?'' she asked.
She took Ben to the shop assistant.
''Don't worry, we'll find your mum,''
said the assistant.

The assistant took Ben on the escalator. They went right to the top floor. Ben cried all the time, "I want my mum!"

They went into a small room. It was full of toys. The assistant gave Ben a teddy.
''I don't want a teddy,'' cried Ben, ''I want my mum!''

''We'll find your mum. What is your name?'' said the assistant.
''Ben,'' said Ben, sniffing. ''Ben Wilson.''
The assistant picked up a microphone.

"Will Mrs Wilson please come to Room 446? Your son Ben is here. Please come to the fourth floor."
Ben's mum heard the message.

Very soon Mum came into the room.
She gave Ben a big hug.
''Dry your eyes,'' said Mum, smiling.
''I'm here now.''

"I was lost," said Ben.
"I'm sorry," said Mum. "So many people came out of the lift."
"I'm sorry too," said Ben. "I will hold your hand tight this time."

Ben and Mum went to have tea. Ben had a milkshake and a big cake.
''Would you have bought me all this if I hadn't got lost?'' asked Ben.
''I don't expect so,'' said Mum, ''but don't you ever get lost again!''